THE DARK SIDE

Werewolves
and Other Shape-Shifters

illustrated by David West
and
written by Anita Ganeri

PowerKiDS
press™
New York

Published in 2011 by The Rosen Publishing Group, Inc.
29 East 21st Street, New York, NY 10010

Designed and produced by
David West Books

Designer and illustrator: David West
Editor: Ronne Randall
U.S. Editor: Kara Murray

Photographic credits: 5t, luc legay; 5m, goldmund100; 5b, Vall; 30 both, coolisandsong24

Library of Congress Cataloging-in-Publication Data

West, David, 1956-
Werewolves and other shapeshifters / illustrated by David West and written by Anita Ganeri.
p. cm. — (The dark side)
Includes bibliographical references (p.   ) and index.
ISBN 978-1-61531-900-8 (library binding) — ISBN 978-1-4488-1572-2 (pbk.) — ISBN 978-1-4488-1573-9 (6-pack)
1. Werewolves — Juvenile literature. 2. Shapeshifting — Juvenile literature. I. Ganeri, Anita, 1961- II. Title.
GR830.W4W47 2011
398'.469 — dc22

2010002661
Manufactured in China

CPSIA Compliance Information: Batch #DS0102PK: For Further Information contact Rosen Publishing, New York, New York at 1-800-237-9932

Contents

Introduction

Many bizarre and gruesome creatures roam the world of mythology. Although their origins may be lost in the mists of history, they have preyed on people's superstitions and imaginations since ancient times. No creatures have struck greater fear than werewolves and other shape-shifters. Caught precariously between the worlds of humans and beasts, they have filled people with terror for centuries and given rise to countless chilling myths and legends told around the world. In modern times, they have been featured in films, fiction, fairy tales, and as characters in comic books and computer games. Are you ready to go over to the dark side? It will send shivers down your spine . . .

Werewolves

A snarling beast, fleet of foot, sly as a fox, and boasting huge claws, a mouth full of foul teeth, and supernatural strength—this is the terrifying werewolf. It roams the countryside in search of prey.

Wolves were hunted because they attacked farmers' livestock.

A werewolf is a creature that can be human or wolf. Sometimes it changed at will and sometimes under the control of another force. It is the best known of the shape-shifters. Most werewolf myths come from medieval times and from countries where packs of wild wolves roamed the countryside and sometimes carried away villagers to eat.

The earliest werewolf tale comes from the classical mythology of ancient Greece. King Lycaon is said to have tried to feed a dead child to the god Zeus, who gets angry and turns Lycaon into a werewolf.

A German print made in 1711 appears to show a werewolf in midtransformation.

Becoming a Werewolf

So how does an unfortunate human become a werewolf in the first place? And once a werewolf, how does he trigger his gruesome transformation from human form to wolf form?

Arching his back in excruciating pain, a werewolf grows a muzzle of sharp teeth, body hair, pointed ears, powerful muscles, and huge claws as he shape-shifts into a wolf.

Modern books and movies often show people becoming werewolves after being bitten or scratched by another werewolf. In mythology, werewolves are created in other ways. Common methods include sleeping outdoors during a full moon, being born under a full moon, and being cursed by a witch. Lycanthropy (the transformation of a human into a wolf) can also be passed from one generation to the next through a family curse.

Folklore in Brazil and Portugal tells that the seventh boy born into a family will be a werewolf. (Sometimes seventh children were abandoned or killed because of this.)

Putting on a wolf-skin belt or an entire wolf skin seem to be the most popular ways for a werewolf to change from human to wolf. When the wolf skin is removed, the process is reversed. Ointments made from ingredients such as nightshade (a poisonous plant) and bat's blood when rubbed on the body also start the transformation. Another trigger is to drink from a puddle in the footprint of a real wolf or from a stream from which a real wolf has drunk. A werewolf may spend hours or even days in wolf form.

A woodcut entitled Werewolf, made in 1512 by Lucas Cranach the Elder, shows the terrifying result of a werewolf attack.

9

Werewolf Features

Both in human and wolf form, werewolves are said to have features of the other form, which allow them to be recognized.

Werewolves are believed to have some strange wolflike features when they are in human form. These include pale, rough skin, bushy eyebrows that grow to meet in the middle, hair on the face, hands, and feet, pointed ears, and long, red fingernails shaped like almonds. One medieval theory was that werewolves wore their wolf skin inside out, with the hair on the inside.

Etchings from a 1667 book, Miraculous Nature, *appear to show male and female werewolves.*

Iconismus . IV. Ponatur è regione pag. 395.

Fig. I Puella pilosa filia annorum duodecim.

Fig. II. Puella pilosa Filia altera annorum octo.

The human eyes of a werewolf behind the face of a wolf.

While in wolf form, mythical werewolves often looked and moved just like real wolves, but they could speak and had human eyes. Other reports tell of werewolves that were half man and half wolf. Any wound inflicted on a werewolf in wolf form would remain when it returned to human form. This was a useful clue for werewolf hunters.

A scene of a werewolf attack from an 1865 book, The Book of Were-Wolves: Being an Account of a Terrible Superstition.
Once in wolf form, a werewolf presented a terrifying shadowy figure that moved swiftly through the countryside.

Warding Off Werewolves

Killing a werewolf with a silver bullet was an idea introduced in eighteenth-century literature.

According to myths, there are various ways to save yourself from a werewolf attack. These are similar to methods of warding off other evil creatures. There are also ways of curing and even killing werewolves.

Traditionally, objects made of the metals iron and silver can be used to ward off an approaching werewolf. Throwing an iron or silver object over a werewolf's head will stop it. Scalding a werewolf with boiling water is also thought to work.

A few types of plants were supposed to stop a werewolf in its tracks. So surrounding a house or campsite with these plants would keep werewolves away during the night. The plants included rye, mistletoe, and wolfsbane. In Belgium, mountain ash was thought to work, too.

According to Greek and Roman myths, keeping a werewolf on the move until it was exhausted would cure it. In medieval Europe, hitting a werewolf on the head three times with a metal knife, piercing its hands with nails, or calling it by its first name three times might do the trick. Killing a werewolf was not easy. You needed to destroy its heart or brain, or shoot it with a silver bullet or arrow. The beast would always return to human form before death.

Aconitum Lycocto, num flore Delphinij.

Aconitum Lycoctonum flore luteo.

Wolfsbane is a popular name for a kind of herb called Aconitum. It has been used for centuries both as a medicine and a poison. It was thought to cause lycanthropy if eaten, but could also repel werewolves.

In Denmark it was believed that boiling water would scare off a werewolf.

Werewolves in Europe

Europe is undoubtedly the world's werewolf hot spot. Here, werewolf myths come from a time when real wolves roamed the length and breadth of the continent, from France to Russia and Norway to Spain.

In the Middle Ages, wolves terrorized rural villages and towns throughout Europe, especially when food was in short supply. Every country has its own word for the werewolf. In Iceland it is *varulfur*, in Italy, *lupo mannero*, and in Lithuania, *vilkatas*. But werewolf tales are rare in Britain, where wolves had been hunted to extinction by early medieval times.

In France, a werewolf is known as a loup-garou (pronounced "loo-guh-ROO"). Perhaps France's most famous werewolf case was of the Beast of Gevaudan. The case began in 1764 with the first of a series of attacks and murders. Terrified survivors spoke of a massive red creature with huge teeth that ran at great speed. Rumors of a werewolf continued even when a huge wolf was trapped and killed.

The Wolf of Chazes was shot and killed in 1765, suspected of being the Beast of Gevaudan. Here it is displayed at the court of King Louis XV.

Waarhafftige Begebenheit!
Mit einem Verbannten Wolff; welcher im 1685sten Jahr im
Marggrafthum Onolzbach etliche Kinder weggetragen und ge-
fressen, lezlich den 9 Octobris in einen brünen zu Neüses, beÿ Eschen-
bach, gefangen, undertödet: so dann dieser figur nach, aufgehangen Worden.

Neüses

Eschenbach

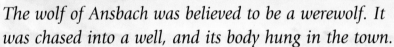

The wolf of Ansbach was believed to be a werewolf. It was chased into a well, and its body hung in the town.

At his trial in Paris in 1598 for the murder of a child, Jacques Rollet admitted that his hands and feet became those of a wolf before he attacked the child. He used ointment to cause the change. Germany's most famous werewolf was Peter Stubbe. Legend says that Stubbe became a wolf and attacked and killed local people. He was finally captured and confessed to becoming a werewolf by wearing a wolf-skin belt. Stubbe was executed in 1589.

The story of Little Red Riding Hood may have had its roots in werewolf myths.

Werewolves Around the World

Although Europe is the main source of werewolf myths, there are werewolf stories from many other parts of the world. Some even originate in places where there have never been real wolves.

In North America, where wolves still roam today, werewolf myths are quite common. In eastern Canada, myths about loups-garous in the forests around Quebec were brought from France by colonists, and were mixed with Native American beliefs. The French also spread their werewolf myths to Haiti and other islands in the Caribbean, and to New Orleans, Louisiana.

A wolf helmet made by the Tlingit people of Alaska, who admired the wolf's strength and hunting skills.

The Crow Indians believed that a spirit in the form of a werewolf lived in Big Horn Canyon and would eat any human who ventured there.

Native North American people have their own werewolf tales to tell. The Algonquian people, a group made up of many Native American tribes, believe in an evil spirit known as the Wendigo. It could turn people into gluttonous, flesh-eating, werewolflike creatures, looking like skeletons with skin. The Navajo thought there were witches who took the form of wolves, known as Mai-Cob.

In northern Argentina, it was believed that if seven sons in a row were born to a family, the seventh would become a werewolf (or *lobizón*). The creature would wander the mountains, surviving by eating dead animals in between attacking humans.

Haiti The Jé-rouge ("red eyes") is a spirit that possesses people, turning them into werewolflike, man-eating creatures.

Brazil Portuguese settlers in South America brought with them myths of the werewolf, or lobisomem.

Mexico The nahual *is a werewolf that steals cheese and attacks women, and can also become a cat, eagle, or bull.*

Philippines The aswang *is part vampire and part werewolf that feeds on human flesh.*

North Africa The bouda *is a type of sorcerer that can be transformed into a were-hyena.*

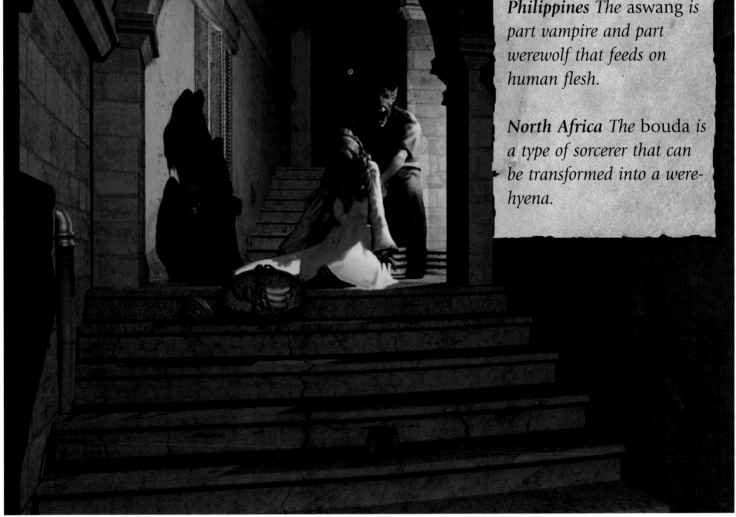

A lobizón drags an unfortunate victim into the shadows of an Argentinian town.

Other Shape-Shifters

There are many other mythical creatures that make terrible transformations, such as the Romanian *strigoi*, a blood-sucking zombie that can change into many different animals, including barn owls, bats, rats, cats, wolves, snakes, and toads.

Daphne, a nymph in Greek mythology, transformed herself into a tree to escape the god Apollo.

In Norse mythology, Fafnir shape-shifted from a dwarf into a dragon, the symbol of greed, to guard a hoard of gold.

Tales of shape-shifters come from countries all over the world. Many are were-beasts, humans who change into animal form just as werewolves change into wolf form and carry out horrifying attacks on victims. Among them are were-cats, such as the were-jaguar of Central America and the were-tiger of India, were-snakes in China, were-crocodiles in Africa, and were-bears in Scandinavia. Vampires were thought to transform into bats or wolves.

In mythology, gods, witches, wizards, sorcerers, and fairies often have the power of shape-shifting. They may take the shape of almost any animal they desire.

Were-Cats

The were-cat is the feline equivalent of the werewolf. Were-cats feature in the mythology of countries where lions, tigers, leopards, and other big cats roam.

Were-tiger myths are common throughout Asia. Undoubtedly the myths are linked to real tiger attacks on people. In China, the victims of curses became were-tigers, as did the ghosts of real tigers.

In Thailand, a tiger that killed lots of people during its mortal life was thought to become a were-tiger when it died.

In India, a were-tiger was thought to be a sorcerer who could take tiger form. Indian were-tigers were thought to have attacked and killed cattle and often stalked and savaged villagers.

In Indonesia, a were-tiger takes its big-cat shape at night to protect its livestock and crops. It rarely attacks humans unless it is very hungry or seeking revenge.

Asian were-tiger

A fearsome were-jaguar leaps from the undergrowth of a jungle.

The were-jaguar was a supernatural creature that terrorized the people of ancient civilizations of Mesoamerica (modern-day southern Mexico and northern Central America) including the Olmecs, Mayas, and Aztecs. A were-jaguar was the master of the forest and was said to transform from human form to jaguar form by putting on the skin of a real jaguar. Many priests and shamans were supposed to be were-jaguars. Images of were-jaguars are common in art of the time, especially the art of the Olmecs.

An Olmec stone carving of a part human and part jaguar creature made sometime between 1000 BC and 300 BC.

Some African peoples believed in lion and leopard gods and goddesses, which took human form and also transformed into lions and leopards. The children of these gods and goddesses become were-lions or were-leopards. Other African peoples believed that members of their royal families became were-lions when they died.

Aztec warriors believed that dressing in jaguar skins gave them the edge in battle. This image comes from the Codex Magliabechiano, an Aztec religious document.

Skin-Walkers and Berserkers

Of all the shape-shifters, none are more terrifying than the crafty skin-walkers of North American legend and the crazed berserkers of Norse myths.

In Native American legends, a skin-walker is a person who can transform into any animal at will. The crow, the fox, the wolf, and the coyote are common forms. A skin-walker takes the form of the animal that is most useful at the time. For example, it might become a crow to gain a bird's-eye view of the land below. Skin-walkers would knock on the doors and windows of houses, terrifying those inside.

In Norse myth, a berserker is a warrior who puts on the skin of a bear (or sometimes a wolf), which transforms him into a fighter with superhuman strength and speed. The word *berserker* is the Old Norse word *ber* (meaning bear) and *serkr* (meaning coat).

The Hombre Caiman (or Alligator Man) of Colombian folklore is a fisherman turned alligator.

The English word *berserk* is derived from it. A berserker fought as though in a terrible rage, striking and biting his enemies, and howling ferociously like a wolf, but he could not be harmed himself.

This bronze plate found on the Swedish island of Öland shows a Viking warrior and a berserker. In reality, berserkers may have fought under the influence of alcohol or drugs.

Skin-walkers moved so fast that they were almost impossible to catch. Bullets had no effect on them.

Swan Maidens and Selkies

A common theme in shape-shifting mythology is an animal that transforms into human form by removing its skin. The creature then appears in the shape of a young woman.

The swan maiden features in Norse myths. By removing its skin, a swan maiden transforms from a swan to a young woman. The transformation is reversed by putting the skin back on or sometimes by dressing in clothes with swan feathers attached. In some stories a young man steals the swan maiden's skin while she is in human form and she marries him so that she can recover her skin.

In the Old Norse poem "Volundarkvida," three brothers marry the swan maidens they see bathing.

Selkies rose from the sea and danced on the shore. Selkies were sometimes forced to marry men who took and hid their sealskins.

Myths that originated in the Orkneys and Shetland islands, both island groups off northern Scotland, describe the selkie, a creature from the sea that sheds its skin to turn from seal form to human form. The selkie must put its sealskin back on to return to seal form. The selkie may only be seen by one human, and only for a short time before it must return to the sea. Similar myths come from the Faroe Islands, Iceland, and Ireland, where seals are often seen.

In Africa, the buffalo maiden is a buffalo that shape-shifts into a young woman. In China, the fox spirit often appears as a girl. Similar myths come from Korea and Japan, where the fox spirit is called a *kitsune*.

The Japanese kitsune *casts a fox-shaped shadow even when in human form.*

Shape-Shifter Gods

Myths from ancient Greece and other ancient civilizations describe gods, goddesses, and demons who change shape to gain an advantage in combat, to play tricks, and to find love.

In Greek mythology, Zeus took the form of different animals, including a cuckoo, a swan, and a bull, to visit goddesses and mortal women. Proteus was known as the Old Man of the Sea. He knew all things, including the future. He would reveal his secrets only to someone who tied him down, which was tricky, since Proteus would take the shape of different animals to escape.

The ancient Egyptian god Seth took many animal forms.

In Norse mythology, Loki is the companion of Odin, god of war. He is a troublemaker who has the ability to change shape, and become any animal. In Hindu mythology, a *naga* is a being that is half human half god who can appear in human or serpent form. In Hindu art, nagas are shown as multiheaded cobras or as creatures with a human head and a coiled serpent body.

In Greek mythology, Europa is carried off to Crete by the god Zeus, disguised in the form of a white bull.

In Homer's Odyssey, *Proteus shape-shifts into a lion to escape the clutches of Menelaus.*

Punished

Gods, goddesses, the Devil, witches, wizards, and sorcerers have often used shape-shifting as a form of punishment. Victims were changed into a whole host of terrible creatures, usually to remain in that form for the rest of their days—or even for all eternity.

A Greek vase showing Circe transforming Odysseus's men into wild pigs.

In Homer's *Odyssey*, the goddess Athena took on many forms. She was also the goddess of handicrafts. When Arachne, a weaver, challenged her to a weaving contest, she changed Arachne into a spider. Artemis, the Greek goddess of wild animals, transformed Actaeon, a Greek hero, into a stag because he saw her bathing. Circe was a Greek sorceress with the power to change people into animals. She transformed Odysseus's men into pigs when they landed on her island.

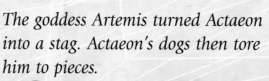

The goddess Artemis turned Actaeon into a stag. Actaeon's dogs then tore him to pieces.

Odin transformed Svipdag into a sea dragon because he had angered him. Later, Svipdag's wife, Freya, tried to rescue him but could not break Odin's spell.

Arachne was transformed into a spider after she angered the goddess Athena.

Russian legend describes the *wawkalak*, a person turned into a werewolf by the Devil as a punishment. Saint Patrick is said to have changed Vereticus, a Welsh king, into a wolf after Vereticus rejected Christianity. In Norse legend, Loki, companion of the gods Odin and Thor, was punished for killing Odin's son. Odin turned one of Loki's sons into a wolf, which promptly ate Loki's other son. Odin also turned the hero Svipdag into a dragon.

Glossary

berserk (ber-SERK) To go into a frenzy of violent or destructive behavior.

classical (KLA-sih-kul) Having to do with the ancient Greeks and Romans and their civilizations.

colonists (KAH-luh-nists) People who settle in a place far from their homeland but that may be ruled by their homeland.

confessed (kun-FESD) Told the truth about something.

coyote (ky-OH-tee) A doglike animal that lives throughout North America.

etchings (ECH-ingz) Drawings made on metal or glass, using acid or a sharp instrument.

executed (EK-suh-kyoot-ed) Put to death.

fleet (FLEET) Quick.

gluttonous (GLUT-nus) Greedy or with a big appetite.

legends (LEH-jendz) Traditional stories, often based on supposedly historical events.

lycanthropy (lih-KANT-thruh-pee) The supposed transformation of a human into a wolf.

medieval (mee-DEE-vul) Relating to the Middle Ages, a period of European history from around the fifth to the fifteenth century.

mortal (MOR-tul) Having to do with living things that do not live forever but eventually die.

myths (MITHS) Traditional stories, not based in historical fact but using supernatural characters to explain human behavior and natural events.

nymph (NIMF) In Greek mythology, it is a spirit in the form of a beautiful girl.

prey (PRAY) Animals that are hunted by other animals for food.

repel (rih-PEL) To force back or drive back.

sorcerer (SAWR-seh-rer) A person who uses magical powers. Another word for a witch or wizard.

supernatural (soo-per-NA-chuh-rul) Having to do with magical beings, such as fairies and ghosts, and unexplained events.

vampire (VAM-py-er) A batlike creature that rises from a grave at night to drink its victims' blood.

zombie (ZOM-bee) A supernatural spirit that brings a dead body back to life.

Further Reading

Boekhoff P.M. *Werewolves. Monsters.* Farmington Hills, MI: KidHaven Press, 2004.

Ganeri, Anita. *An Illustrated Guide to Mythical Creatures.* New York, NY: Hammond, 2009.

Godfrey, Linda S. and Rosemary Ellen Guiley. *Werewolves. Mysteries, Legends, and Unexplained Phenomena.* New York, NY: Chelsea House Publishers, 2008.

Krensky, Stephen. *Werewolves. Monster Chronicles.* Minneapolis, MN: Lerner Publishing Group, 2006.

Ollhoff, Jim. *Werewolves. The World of Horror.* Edina, MN: ABDO & Daughters, 2007.

Oxlade, Chris. *Can Science Solve the Mystery of Vampires and Werewolves?* Chicago, IL: Heinemann-Raintree, 2008.

Werewolf attacking a man, from a fifteenth-century German work

Index

Web Sites

Due to the changing nature of Internet links, PowerKids Press has developed an online list of Web sites related to the subject of this book. This site is updated regularly. Please use this link to access the list:
www.powerkidslinks.com/darkside/werewolf/